THE ST
COLO
WINES

BY ABBOTT FAY

WESTERN REFLECTIONS PUBLISHING COMPANY®

Montrose, CO

First Edition
Printed in the United States of America

ISBN 1-890437-73-5

Cover photograph by Art Fox, Rocky Mountain Scenics
Text design by Laurie Goralka Design

Western Reflections Publishing Company®
P.O. Box 1647
Montrose, CO 81402
www.westernreflectionspub.com

Dedicated to
Ann Seewald
and the memory of Jim Seewald
who, with Mary and Gerald Ivancie,
founded the Colorado wine industry.

Table of Contents

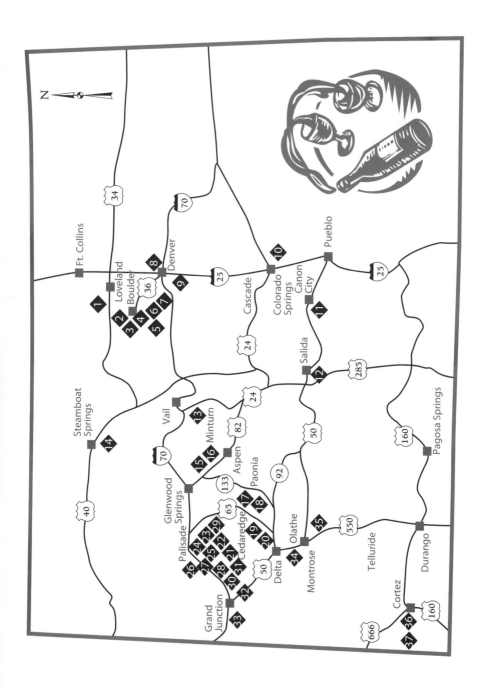

Colorado Wineries

1   Trail Ridge Winery
2   Augustina's Winery
3   BookCliff Vineyards
4   Redstone Meadery
5   Creekside Cellars
6   Spero Winery
7   Old Town Winery
8   J.A. Balistreri Vineyards
9   Avanti Winery
10 Pike's Peak Vineyards Winery
11 Holy Cross Abbey
12 Mountain Spirit Winery
13 Miniturn Cellars
14 Steamboat Springs Cellars
15 Baharav Vineyards
16 Aspen Valley Winery
17 Terror Creek Winery
18 Puesta Del Sol Winery
19 Stoney Mesa Winery

20 Surface Creek Winery
21 Colorado Cellars Winery
22 Carlson Vineyards
23 Corley Vineyards
24 Canyon Wind Cellars
25 St. Kathryn Cellars
26 Grande River Vineyards
27 Plum Creek Cellars
28 Confre Cellars: Rocky Mountain Meadery &
    Rocky Mountain Cidery
29 DeBeque Canyon Winery
30 Graystone Vineyards
31 Garfield Estates Winery
32 Reeder Mesa Vineyards
33 Two Rivers Winery
34 Cottonwood Cellars, Inc.
35 Rocky Hill WInery
36 Guy Drew Vineyards
37 Sutcliffe Vineyards

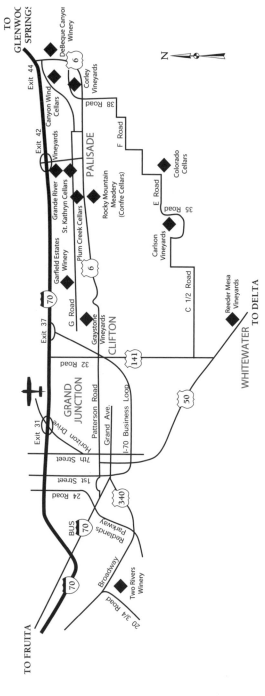

Grand Valley Wineries

"Our Vines Have Tender Grapes"

Song of Solomon

*W*ine has been produced in Colorado since the earliest territorial days in the 1860s. While most of these early wines were made for home consumption from grapes grown on local farms or in residential gardens, some were sold to neighbors.

Along the Front Range, a few areas enjoyed seasons that were usually favorable to growing Concord grapes, which could then be made into sweet wines. However there were always the threats of late spring frosts or early autumn freezing temperatures. As if that weren't enough, a summer hailstorm could also wreak havoc to the vineyard. Nevertheless, in the eastern foothills of the Rocky Mountains, vineyards near Penrose and Cañon City often came up with good quality wine grapes, which had been planted from European stock.

While wine was popular in those earliest years, prospectors, trappers, traders, and cattlemen often preferred whiskey. As Dorothy Parker was credited with writing a century later, "Wine is fine, but liquor is quicker." The most famous (or infamous) of those early whiskeys was known as "Taos Lightnin'." Simeon Turley produced one version of the potent liquor; and one of his descendents, Rick Turley, would later become a major producer of Colorado wines.

No grapes were grown on the western slope of Colorado during the 1860s and 1870s, since according to a treaty signed in 1864, the Ute Indians were to have ownership of the majority of the land west of the Continental Divide in Colorado forever. When precious metals were discovered in the San Juan Mountains, the Utes agreed to allow prospectors into a few selected places in those mountains, which eventually led to the founding of such white settlements as Lake City, Silverton, and Ouray. The settlers who came to the Western Slope soon discovered that some of the area's valleys had excellent agricultural prospects.

The Utes themselves were not farmers; they were mostly hunters and gatherers. In the 1870s, there were only about 5,000 of them occupying an area stretching from what are today the towns of Craig south to New Mexico, and Gunnison west to the Utah border. Among these natives, there were at least five distinctly different bands with no real sense of unification.

When the White River Utes of Northwestern Colorado revolted against the inept and arrogant agent Nathan C. Meeker in 1879, he and seven other agency men were killed in what came to be called the "Meeker Massacre." The white people were just looking for an excuse to get the Utes out of Colorado. Thus the cry went up, "The Utes Must Go!"

The original government plans called for the Southern Utes to be confined to reservations along the New Mexico border. Those in the central and northern areas were to be forced into a reservation in the Grand Valley (now the Grand Junction region); and, according to the Ute treaty, "if sufficient agricultural land wasn't found there," they were to be moved into adjoining lands in Utah.

When the white leaders came to realize that the Grand Valley not only had good agricultural land but actually had the longest growing season (180 days) in Colorado, only the second part of the plan was enacted, and the Ute natives were evacuated to northeastern Utah. This was accomplished in September of 1881 and heralded a land rush into the vast former Ute territory. Farmers, ranchers, and others scrambled into the warm valleys of western Colorado to "stake their claims."

By the spring of 1882 settlers were bringing fruit and grapevine stocks to such favored locations as the new settlements of Paonia and Hotchkiss, which were located on the North Fork of the Gunnison River, and also to the Grand Valley (at that time the river now known as the Colorado was named the Grand). It was a good choice as verified by the fact that at the present, these two regions are Colorado's only U.S. certified viticultural areas, in which estate wines (which must pass from vine to bottle under a single control) may be so labeled. They are known as the "Grand Valley" and the "West Elk Mountain" regions, after being designated as such by the Bureau of Alcohol, Tobacco, and Firearms after painstaking research. Ninety-five percent of Colorado wine grapes are grown in these two areas.

Rapid Creek, which flows into the Colorado River at the western mouth of DeBeque Canyon near present-day Palisade, was probably the first area in western Colorado to have grape vines planted. Frank Marlot, John Goffredi, and the Kladdock Family grew their wine grapes there. Soon thereafter, the area across the river from Palisade became known as "the Vinelands," a name it retains even to the present day. By 1885, the first grapes from these areas had been harvested and made into home-fermented wine.

The Palisade area has always been one of the finest wine-growing areas in Colorado.

Photo Courtesy of the Palisade Chamber of Commerce.

One of the reasons the Vinelands was such a favorable location was that nearby Mount Lincoln and Mount Garfield retained the heat of the day and reflected it into the valley below, thus providing for longer frost-free seasons. Water was plentiful despite a total annual precipitation that averaged only about nine inches, because water from the Grand (now Colorado) River was redirected into irrigation canals that were built only after an amazing amount of backbreaking labor. Their construction meant that farmers no longer had to carry water in pails up from the river to nurse the struggling vines.

In the 1880s and 1890s there was a substantial colony of Italian railroad workers in Grand Junction who wanted easily available wine. They planted at least one vineyard on the southern uplands of the Grand Valley, an area now known as the Redlands. This land hovers beneath the spectacular natural pyramids, domes, and gigantic obelisks that are now contained in the Colorado National Monument. There are a few producing grapevines on the Redlands that are said to be over eighty years of age.

There was no evidence of a wine industry at that time, although some trading of farm products was present. Peach farmers found that these same warm and dry conditions around the town of Palisade produced some of the finest peaches in America. On East Orchard Mesa there were splendid apples, plums, pears, and peaches, all of which could be blended with grape juice and fermented.

Fruits from the North Fork of the Gunnison River were soon exported, and they even took first place in every category at the 1893 Columbian Exposition in Chicago. It was such an honor that fruit ranches near Hotchkiss are still called "Gold Medal Orchards."

By 1901 a railroad had been built to bring coal out from the mining town of Somerset, located on the upper North Fork of the Gunnison River above Paonia. The Italian miners working at Somerset wanted wine, but the town was too high in altitude to grow grapes. As there was no road through the narrow canyon to Somerset (only a railroad), grapes grown in Paonia were left about halfway to Somerset at a store near the railroad in the village of Bowie. Miners would then ride their horses down river along the rails to pick up the grapes and take them home to make wine.

The Women's Christian Temperance Union became very active in Colorado at the beginning of the twentieth century, with anti-saloon groups being established in most towns and cities. Mesa County, the main site of the future Colorado wine industry, went dry in 1909. By 1916 the State of Colorado as a whole had adopted prohibition, four years before the United States as a whole "took the pledge" in the form of the Eighteenth Amendment. As a result of Prohibition, many grapevines in the Grand Valley were uprooted, and the Palisade area was re-planted — mostly in peaches.

Even during Prohibition farmers were permitted to make forty gallons of grape juice for personal use from their vines; and with a bit of deliberate neglect or perhaps an additional touch of yeast, the sugar in the juice fermented; so the area was not entirely dry. Federal agents made a few arrests and levied a few fines, but the local law-enforcement agencies were not very attentive to the problem. Meantime, many of the nearby mountain communities made illegal whiskey to sell in Colorado cities from stills hidden in home cellars or in the rugged nearby mountains.

As prohibition failed throughout the nation (with even President Harding imbibing) the "noble experiment" was abandoned in 1933. By that time excellent cherries and apples were being shipped nationwide from Paonia. Palisade peaches were designated by name in some of New York City's most famous hotels and restaurants and were even found on trans-Atlantic luxury liners. The Western Slope fruit farmers were doing just fine selling their award-winning fruit, so why would they bother to go back to growing wine grapes? Actually, it took almost half a century before they did.

The Renaissance

Dr. Gerald Invancie and Jim Seewald were the founders of Colorado's modern wine industry.

Ivancie, a periodontist by profession, was born in 1923 to Slavic parents and grew up in a family that had an appreciation of fine wines. As a hobby, he experimented as an adult with different methods to produce better wines. Invancie moved from his

Dr. Gerald Ivancie, one of Colorado's wine pioneers.
Photo Courtesy of Ivancie Cellars

Minnesota home to Denver, Colorado in 1958. It was there he realized that the high altitude and dry climate were advantageous in both of the important processes of wine manufacture: quicker evaporation and more efficient aging.

His wine products were very much in demand among his friends; so his wife, Mary, suggested that they work together to create a winemaking business. The result was the first commercial winery in Colorado, which was located at 400 S. Lipan Street in Denver. The Ivancies began marketing their original wines, made from California grapes, in 1969.

The next year the Ivancies entered four of their sample wines in the International Wine Fair at Ljubljana, Yugoslavia. They were stunned, but delighted, when informed that all four of their entries were awarded silver medals, the second highest possible distinctions.

Dr. Gerald and Mary Ivancie with some of their award-winning wines.
Photo Courtesy of Ivancie Cellars

IVANCIE CELLARS

Zinfandel

1968

PRODUCED AND BOTTLED BY IVANCIE WINES, INC.,
DENVER, COLORADO BW3
ALCOHOL 13% BY VOLUME

Courtesy of Jane Foster

9

Their prize-winning wines were Chenin Blanc, Cabernet Sauvignon, Zinfandel, and Granny Rose Sec. That same year, their Pinot Blanc and Petite Syrah creations won silver medals at the Los Angeles County Fair in Pomona, California, edging out many of the long-established California wines!

The major advisor to the Ivancie enterprise was Warren Winiarski, a California consultant, who later founded the popular White Stags Leap Wine Cellars in that state. When bad weather severely damaged the California crops in 1972, the price of grapes skyrocketed. Winiarski then took a good careful look at the Grand Valley of Colorado as a more reliable source of grapes.

A bad freeze in the winter of 1962-63 had destroyed many of the trees trees in the famed peach orchards of the Palisade area. Ivancie and Winiarski talked Palisade High School agricultural teacher, Curtis Talley, into trying out wine grapes as they were a hardier crop, because they bud later than fruit trees.

The first commercial wine grape planters in the Grand Valley, in addition to Talley, were George Zimmerman, Ken Schmidt, Fred (Danny) Bracken, and Ralph Blatnick, all of the upper valley around Palisade, and Jim Gigoux of the Redlands, which is located south and west of Grand Junction.

In 1973, after contracting to share the winery's profits with the growers, Ivancie sold the business to Jerry Shaw and another group of co-investors. Shaw sought to quickly swing into a larger production; but that move proved disastrous, and Ivancie Wines closed in 1975.

For years, Jim and Ann Seewald had operated a winemaking business as a hobby in Denver, which attracted many home wine enthusiasts. Ivancie and Seewald were close friends, sharing many ideas about grape growing and wine making. When the Grand Valley growers were left without a Colorado winery, they considered returning the land to fruit orchards; but Ivancie and Seewald had other ideas for the area.

At about the same time the United States government, through a "Four Corners Regional Commission," established a research project to examine alternative sources of income for farmers in the Southwest. The agency gave a grant to Colorado State University, which was to be used for the exploration of wine grape cultivation; and that institution, in turn, established research centers on Orchard

Mesa near Palisade and in the area of the North Fork of the Gunnison River. These efforts led to Colorado State making optimistic predictions of profitable vineyard production in both locations.

In 1980 Seewald gathered together a group of eighteen wine enthusiasts to invest in a winery near Palisade. Thus was created Colorado Mountain Vineyards. Although the name was later changed to Colorado Cellars, it is the oldest winery now operating in Colorado.

Seewald's son, Doug, who studied viticulture with experts in Washington

Jim Seewald, the other founder of the Colorado wine industry.

Photo Courtesy of Ann Seewald

State, also set out a Riesling vineyard known as Cobble Hill Vineyards. It was located next to the winery. Seewald bought grapes from a constantly increasing number of Grand Valley vineyards; and with his expertise as a winemaker, Colorado Mountain Vineyards was an instant success.

Between 1984 and 1993 Seewald's wines were given more than fifteen awards and commendations nationwide. The Colorado wine industry was beginning to savor the sweet (and dry) taste of success!

Veteran viticulturalist Wade Wolfe was employed by the government to promote better grape harvests in Colorado. In addition to the Palisade area, he visited growers in Cañon City, Penrose, Hotchkiss, and Paonia.

Ann and Jim Seewald were responsible for the exhaustive efforts of research and the official request process that ultimately resulted in the recognition by Federal officials of the Grand Valley Viticultural Area.

Colorado Cellars lets its customers know it is Colorado's oldest winery.

Author Photo

In the wake of the infamous stock market plunge of 1987, additional investors backed out of their support of the Seewald winery, which forced a sale of Colorado Mountain Vineyards. The winery fell into the hands of Tom Husband, who retained Seewald as his winemaker. Husband desired to sell more wines east of the Rockies, but his venture also failed. Western Slope wine salesman, Rick Turley, bought the winery and gave it the current name of Colorado Cellars, initially retaining Seewald as winemaker. However there were disagreements regarding methods and philosophy, so Seewald decided to retire in 1992.

By that time, other Colorado wineries were flourishing. Plum Creek Cellars was originally started in Larkspur, south of Castle Rock, but it was later moved to Palisade. In 1984 Mary and Parker Carlson had begun making wine at their vineyards on East Orchard Mesa. Stephen Smith, a petroleum land specialist and home winemaker from Denver, had established the Grande River Vineyards in the 1990s. This vineyard is now the largest grower of wine grapes in Colorado. On the Front Range, Pike's Peak Vineyards in Colorado Springs, which had been licensed a decade earlier, had been producing wines from foothill grapes with varying success, depending a great deal on the weather conditions.

In the North Fork Valley of the Gunnison River, in Delta County, several vineyards had been planted in the early 1990s. Most, but not all, growers sold their grapes to Plum Creek Cellars. By 1993 Terror Creek Winery near Paonia sold its first vintage. Three years later, S. Rhodes was producing elite wines near Hotchkiss.

Then after much research and documentation, growers Barbara and Mike Heck were able to get certification for Colorado's second viticultural region, the West Elk Mountains, in 2001. It received its name from the West Elk Mountain Range, which overlooks the high altitude growing areas of the North Fork Valley. Colorado wines were now firmly established.

Colorado wines are now considered some of the best in the United States.

Photo Courtesy of Bob C. Dougherty, Palisade Tribune

Fine grapes from Corley Vineyards.

Author Photo

*Parker Carlson of
Carlson Vineyards
of Palisade.*

Author Photo

Colorado Art
in a Bottle

*W*ines are like any other form of art. Some people like folk art, others prefer traditional or classic forms. Some individuals are advocates of nature; others prefer abstract, realism, or impressionism.

Most specialists seem to agree that a good wine is any wine you like. Wines that have won double high awards may not taste good to your palate; some that are scorned by the connoisseurs may become your own favorite. Each person has a special combination of taste buds, an equally personal olfactory system to react to the aroma, and a distinct idea of how a wine should feel in the mouth.

Even the fact that a certain wine is a best seller in a given winery does not mean that you'll like it. The quality of a wine is not determined by democratic votes; each person is the autocrat of his own preference.

Doug Caskey, Secretary of the Colorado Wine Industry Development Board, judging an amateur entry.
Photo Courtesy of Bob C. Dougherty, Palisade Tribune

16

Some wines are kept in oak casks for many years; others are removed early to prevent an "oaky" taste, and others are fermented in stainless steel. A legend, which is frequently told, concerns three monks who were tasting wine from a single keg. One declared that there was a hint of leather in the taste. The second monk said he detected instead a taste of pine. The third declared absolutely that he strongly tasted metal in the wine. When the keg was emptied, it was found that in the bottom of the keg there was a metal skeleton key tied by a leather thong to a wooden identification tag made of pine! How sensitive can individual taste be?

Gina Jerome judging fine Colorado wines.
Photo Courtesy of Bob C. Dougherty, Palisade Tribune

For that reason, this writer makes no evaluation of the quality of any wine, except to mention a few awards given in national and international wine tasting and to comment in general on the superior quality of the grapes grown in Colorado.

A word about awards: In what is known as "blind tasting," a panel (usually composed of four experts) is given a variety of unmarked wines. If all agree on the best of the type, it is awarded a gold medal. It is then given to another team without knowledge of the previous rating. If that group also decides the same wine is the best of all, the result is a "double gold."

Variety is the keynote of Colorado's thirty-seven wineries. Each vintner creates his or her own artistic product. None of the wines are mass-produced; each is a reflection of the meticulous care of the vineyard, the timing of the harvest, and the subsequent crushing, fermentation, and aging. The writer has found that no two Colorado winemakers agree completely on any of these factors.

In ancient Rome the wine considered best by the winemaker was designated by hanging a sprig of holly above it. Practical philosopher, Pubilius Syrus, wrote in the first century, B.C.: "You need not hang up the ivy branch over the wine that will sell."

Every Colorado winemaker interviewed noted that all the wines they made had sold out.

*Scott Panko as Bacchus, Greek God of Wine, at the
Colorado Mountain Wine Festival at Palisade.
Photo Courtesy of Bob C. Dougherty,* Palisade Tribune

The Lowdown on
the Up High

The character of wine depends on three factors: the nature of the soil, the general type of climate, and the variety of the wine being cultivated.

The quality of the wine, however, depends on the vintage, which is greatly influenced by the weather conditions encountered during the individual growing season. High altitudes and a consistent climate give a distinct advantage to the majority of vineyards in Colorado.

The two officially designated viticultural areas of the Grand Valley and the North Fork of the Gunnison River (officially the West Elk Region), and a few others fit these general requirements for quality. Among the other areas are the Surface Creek Valley in Delta County, a wine-growing region near the town of Olathe, and McElmo Canyon in the southwestern corner of Colorado.

Plenty of Colorado sunshine furnishes warm days and cool nights during the grape growing season. The soil, however, demands some struggle to produce the best flavors. In the Grand Valley, geological formations such as the Bookcliff Range and the monoliths of Colorado National Monument, act as reflecting agents to lengthen the warmth of the day and producing a longer growing season. Canyon winds also waft over the vines to lessen the effects of late spring or early autumn frosts.

Especially important is the water supply to the vines. Many of the wine growing regions in the world are dependent solely upon rainfall, often too little or too much, to determine the quality of the vintage year. In the Grand Valley, total annual precipitation is less than nine inches. To grow any crop irrigation is needed, but this allows the grower to control exactly the best possible amount of water that will reach the vines. Some growers use well-drained surface irrigation; others use overhead sprinklers to duplicate the effect of rain. Drainage is important. The rule is: "Grape vines do not like wet feet."

Wonderful Colorado wine grapes — ready for harvest.
Photo Courtesy of Bob C. Dougherty, Palisade Tribune

For that reason it may be said that every year is a vintage year in Western Colorado. Only some rare weather disaster could disprove that statement, such as a calamitous late frost that could defy even the warm canyon winds. Yet even then, wind generators are often used to save at least part of the crop.

Under such conditions the sugar content of the grape itself is enhanced, and the distinct flavor of each variety is well preserved. Because of the low relative humidity, the comparative lack of mildew formation is another real asset of growing grapes in Colorado.

In August, as the grapes begin to mature, the grower must also protect the vineyards from another danger — attacks by hungry birds. Usually covering the rows of vines with netting prevents their eating the fruit. Other devices include timed blasts or recorded tapes that imitate the birds' own sounds warning of nearby predators.

Picking up tasting glasses at the Palisade Wine Festival.
Photo Courtesy of Bob C. Dougherty, Palisade Tribune

The Winemakers

None of the Colorado wineries engage in the mass-production of wine for national consumption. As many wine experts have pointed out, small wineries frequently have excellent products because of the detailed care given to each stage of growing, crushing, fermentation, and aging. To make wine, the grapes are first crushed in a wine press. The grape skins are left in the juice of red or pink varieties and are removed for white wines. Then the fluid is stored in tanks to allow fermentation to take place, both from natural sugars and, usually, through the addition of yeast to the grape juice. At the right moment, the wine is poured into wooden casks for proper aging. There is little need to add an exorbitant amount of sulfur to Colorado wines to prolong their shelf life, as almost all of the wines produced in Colorado are sold out each year.

The congenial respect shown by each winemaker in regard to competitors in the Colorado wine market is remarkable. Many are very complimentary of the products that may be made for different styles and tastes. The Wine Industry Board of Colorado was formed by legislative action at the request of the vintners over two decades ago. It provides funds for constant research, promotes sales in Colorado, and advertises Colorado wines in a few national publications.

Many Colorado wines contain more than just grapes. There are fruit wines, berry wines, and honey wines (mead), as well as various combinations.

The wineries themselves are often major attractions. While a few winemakers only sell directly to distributors and select restaurants, the majority of the Colorado wineries have tasting rooms. There are also fine restaurants in some of the wineries, and some have facilities for meetings or even small conventions. Others feature outdoor musical events in the summer and autumn months. One even has a bed and breakfast accommodation.

Colorado wines have been featured on the AMTRAK trains that run between Denver and Grand Junction. The famed American Orient Express has also included Colorado wine tours in its destinations. Some of the state's most distinguished restaurants feature the Colorado wines. In Mesa County the local wineries have proven to be a most popular tourist attraction, second only to the spectacular Colorado National Monument. Professional tour operators often include wine tastings on their circuits of Colorado.

Regarding each of the vintners, it is hard to resist the words of Omar Khayyam in his *Rubaiyat:*

> *"I often wonder what the*
> *vintners buy*
> *One half as precious as*
> *what they sell."*

Here are the stories of each winery in the approximate chronological order of their first offerings, together with a short history of the devoted people who created the wonderful products of which they can be rightfully proud.

Palisade produces its own fruit and wine guide.

Photo Courtesy of the
Palisade Chamber of Commerce

Rick Turley, owner of Colorado Cellars in Palisade.
Author Photo

The Doyen of Colorado Wineries

COLORADO CELLARS WINERY
3553 E Road
Palisade 81526

*J*im Sewell, together with a group of enthusiasts whom he came to know from his hobby winemaking shop in Denver, founded what is now the state's oldest winery at Golden in 1978. Colorado grapes were used at the new Colorado Mountain Vineyards; and Gerald Invancie soon closed his earlier winery, which had used California grapes, in support of the new enterprise.

Two years later, Colorado Mountain Vineyards moved to its current location on East Orchard Mesa near Palisade. When Rick Turley later purchased the winery, the name was changed to Colorado Cellars.

While the Colorado Mountain Vineyards' wines had won numerous awards, Turley decided that many of the contests were not very significant, so he discontinued the practice of entering judged tastings. Nevertheless, his wines have totally sold out every year.

According to Turley, Colorado wines, because of their quick turnover, can get by with very little, if any, sulfur being added; as opposed to the mass-marketed wines, which use that element to preserve the flavor for long periods of time.

In addition to a vast variety of grape wines, Colorado Cellars makes wines from plums and cherries. No coloring or flavoring is added to their wines.

Colorado Cellars' wines are marketed statewide. There is also a tasting room and picnic area at the winery itself, which is open weekdays and Saturday afternoons. Call 800-848-2812 for more information.

Plenty of fine wine at a wine tasting from St. Kathryn Cellars.
Photo Courtesy of Bob C. Dougherty, Palisade Tribune

From the Old Homestead

PIKE'S PEAK VINEYARDS WINERY
3901 Janitell Road
Colorado Springs 81201

ruce and Taffy McLaughlin, along with three other investors, founded the Pike's Peak Vineyards Winery at Colorado Springs in 1981. The McLaughlins were experienced winemakers, as they had started growing wine grapes a decade earlier on land owned by Bruce's family in Connecticut.

Taffy fell heir to an old homestead at the edge of Colorado Springs. It had for many decades been the Stinton Dairy, but as the city grew, it was no longer suitable as a home for cows.

Forty acres of wine grapes were planted at the old dairy and were supplemented by grapes from vineyards located near Penrose and Olney Springs. When a hailstorm wiped out their own grapes, the McGlaughlins began to use grapes from the Western Slope of Colorado.

Recently, Pike's Peak Vineyards has set out new plantings, frost-free Chandler reds, which have managed to survive well in the cold areas of New York State.

Producing between 5,000 and 10,000 gallons of wine a year, their label is sold throughout Colorado, other states, and overseas. Paul Tafoya is the manager of the winery.

In addition to the winery, the grounds include a golf course and an amphitheater, where the first three Colorado winefests were held back in 1985, 1986, and 1987.

A restaurant at the winery is open for dinner Tuesday through Saturday evenings. In addition to a tasting room at the winery, the McLaughlins own Taste of Colorado at Cascade, a store which offers a wide variety of Colorado wines for tasting and purchase. They also own the Minturn Cellars, discussed separately in this book.

To find your way to Pike's Peak Vineyards Winery, located across from the "World Arena," call 719-576-0075.

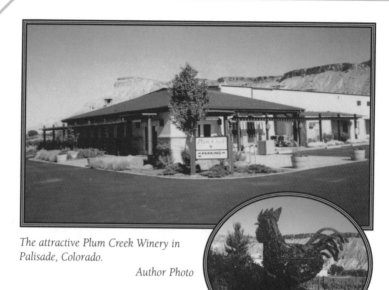

The attractive Plum Creek Winery in
Palisade, Colorado.

Author Photo

The *"Chardonnay Chicken,"*
by sculptor Lyle Nichols, is an
easy way to spot Plum Creek
Cellars.

Author Photo

Behind the Chardonnay Chicken

PLUM CREEK CELLARS
3708 G Road
Palisade 81526

*D*oug and Sue Phillips' Plum Creek Cellars has produced some of the most publicized award-winning wines in Colorado. The Phillips, both attorneys, founded their winery at the town of Larkspur, near Plum Creek, in 1984. They moved their operation to the Western Slope in 1990.

The Plum Creek wines that won double gold medals in international competition, were the *Grand Mesa* in 1992 and the *Cabernet Franc* in both 1997 and 1998. No less than twenty-five of the Plum Creek wines have won gold medals.

Among the experts who helped the Phillips get started was the nationally famous Erik Brunner, who became a specialist in Colorado winemaking. He helped to train Jeanne Baldwin, the current winemaker for Plum Creek.

Especially praised in the nationwide press is their *Redstone Chardonnay.* After wine expert Michael Lonsford of the *Houston Chronicle* and some of his friends blind-tasted Chardonnays, including those from France, California, Australia, Italy, and New Zealand, they found the best of all was the Redstone! Popular novelist Clive Cussler has even included praise for Plum Creek Cellars wine in his book, *Shock Wave.*

Plum Creek has its own on-site vineyards, but the Phillips also use grapes from the Terror Creek Vineyards, located at 6,418 feet above sea level, near Paonia. The *Riesling Ice* wine is extra sweet because it is produced from just-frozen grapes.

The winery itself has a pleasant tasting room furnished with antique furniture, hand-woven rugs, and fine art from the Phillips' collection. It is very easy to spot because the huge "Chardonnay Chicken" steel sculpture by Lyle Nichols that stands boldly in front of the winery.

Plum Creek wines have been served at Mickey Mantle's Sports Bar in New York City. They are also found in some Denver restaurants and can be obtained in a tasting room at Tewksbury & Co. in Writer's Square, across from Larimer Square, in downtown Denver.

The numbers to call for more details are 970-464-7586 or 303-825-1805.

The Carlson Vineyards winery at Christmas time.
Author Photo

Carlson Vineyards' **Cougar Run Merlot/Shiraz** is a full-flavored red blend of Colorado grown Merlot (81%) and Shiraz (19%) grapes. This Merlot/Shiraz has aromas of strawberry jam, blackberry, anise and light smoke. The flavors are reminiscent of berries, anise, black licorice and vanilla. Enjoy the soft mouth feel, full tannins and great finish. Match this wine with red meats, rich fish, pasta, cheese and good friends. Serve at cool room temperature.

Carlson Vineyards, a small "Colorado Grown" farm winery, produces quality grape and fruit wines in the heart of the Western Slope above Palisade, Colorado on East Orchard Mesa.

Mary and Parker Carlson invite you to tour the winery, open seven days a week, and sample our selection of wines. For more information, please call 888-464-5554 or visit www.carlsonvineyards.com.

CARLSON VINEYARDS
COUGAR RUN

1998
GRAND VALLEY

Merlot/Shiraz
81%   19%

COLORADO GROWN
Alcohol 14.5% by Volume

Prairie Dogs, Dinosaurs, and Cougars

CARLSON VINEYARDS
461 35 Road
Palisade 81526

*M*any wine lovers agree that the winery of Parker and Mary Carlson is one of the most congenial places in Colorado to taste the vintages. Only a shingle by the road designates the former packing shed that is now home to some of the most popular Colorado wines. However Parker points out that just following the yellow center line on the paved road through East Orchard Mesa will bring you to the Carlson Vineyards.

A 1964 graduate of the Colorado School of Mines, Parker worked for Coors Ceramics, eventually coming to Grand Junction and founding the fourth oldest winery in the state. He and Mary planted the vineyard in 1981.

Their blends of wine include many fruits and are given very creative names. As the Grand Valley is noted for dinosaur digs, the Carlson's Lemberger wine is called *Tyrannosaurus Red.*

The Carlsons are cat lovers and have on the premises a greeting cat and a guard cat, and they even sell catnip at the winery. A recent trip to the Petrified Forest in Arizona led to their viewing an ancient petroglyph of a cougar. One of their most popular wines, a Merlot-Shiraz blend, now comes with a *Cougar Run* label, with a duplication of the Arizona rock art.

Parker has served as president of the Rocky Mountain Association of Vintners and Viticulturalists.

On the route to Carlson Vineyards from Palisade, one passes the sculpture garden of Lyle Nichols, whose metal creations are displayed throughout the county. On a whimsy, Lyle put up a sign that read: "Sunny Dale Nudist Colony One Mile Ahead." Carlsons stood a naked mannequin in their vineyard, causing motorists to pause for a second glance.

If you want to drop in at the winery (they say they call everyone a visitor, not a customer) and need help, telephone 970-464-5554.

The *"Napa Valley Style"* Grand River winery and vineyards.

Author Photo

Stephen Smith, owner of Grand River Vineyards.

Author Photo

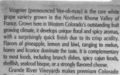

Viognier (pronounced Vee-oh-nyay) is the rare white grape variety grown in the Northern Rhone Valley of France. Grown here in Western Colorado's outstanding fruit growing climate, it develops unique floral and spicy aromas, with a surprisingly quick finish due to its crisp acidity. Flavors of pineapple, lemon and kiwi, ranging to melon, honey and licorice dominate the taste. It is complementary to most foods, including brunch dishes, spicy cajun foods, shellfish, seafood bisque, or a strongly flavored cheese.

Grande River Vineyards makes premium Colorado Grown Wines in traditional styles exclusively from grapes grown on our Mesa de Colorado farms. The name Grande River was chosen to reflect the importance to our valley of the Colorado River (originally known as the Grand) and to show the historic and present day tie of our area to the American Southwest. To learn where you can purchase our wines, call us nationwide at 1-800-CO GROWN (264-7696) or locally 970-464-5867. Visit our website at www.granderiverwines.com or stop by our winery at I-70 exit 42 in Palisade, Colorado.

For your assurance of a 100% Colorado wine experience, look for the phrase "Colorado Grown" on the bottle, which by law, can only be used on wine made from 100% Colorado grown grapes or fruit.

Grande River VINEYARDS

1998
**GRAND VALLEY
ESTATE BOTTLED**

VIOGNIER

Colorado Grown
Mesa de Colorado Farms

GROWN, PRODUCED AND BOTTLED BY GRANDE RIVER VINEYARDS
PALISADE, COLORADO   BW-CO-17
ALCOHOL 13% BY VOLUME • CONTAINS SULFITES

How About Sixty Acres?

GRANDE RIVER VINEYARDS
787 Elberta Avenue
Palisade 81526

*B*efore getting into the wine business, Stephen Smith was an oil and gas land procurement specialist in Denver who also loved good wine. In 1986 he and two geologist friends purchased vineyards near Palisade from pioneer grower, Bennett Price.

Today, Grande River Vineyards has grown to about sixty acres of vineyards, about half the acreage wrapping around the winery, located just off Interstate Highway 70. In addition to his own needs, Smith supplies about half the grapes used in all other Colorado wineries.

Architect Nathan Good designed the winery building, which is reminiscent of Napa Valley, California structures. The beautiful vineyards and winery lure travelers off the Interstate at Exit 42. An average of 200 people a day stop to sample the vintages and, perhaps, use the picnic area. During the summer and fall months, weekly concerts are performed on the spacious grounds at the sunset hours.

Grande River's most popular wine is Merlot, followed by Chardonnay and Meritage Red, a blend of Bordeaux varieties. The *1997 Merlot* won double gold medals in three international competitions. The first gold awarded the Merlot was by the *Dallas Morning News* in 1992, only the fifth year of Grande River production.

An inviting tasting room tempts visitors to cool off on hot summer days with wines that may include *Avalanche Rose, Alpenglo Riesling, Estate White,* and *Pinot Gris.* There is also a banquet room for parties. If you are scheduling an event or just want to know more information, call 970-464-4867 or 800-CO-GROWN.

The winery at Minturn Cellars is located in what once was a narrow alley.
Author Photo

Ted Dunn is ready to greet customers at Minturn Cellars.
Author Photo

Tastes for Skiing and Snowboarding

MINTURN CELLARS
107 Williams Street
Minturn 81645

*M*inturn was for more than a century an important railroad town, a spot where extra locomotives were added to trains to help them make it over the Continental Divide. A large roundhouse was the center of life there. It was also a notable shipping point for the nearby hardrock mines.

The railroad no longer operates through Minturn, and the mines have closed. Taking their place nearby (economically at least) is the largest winter sports complex in the United States — Vail. Now there is a revival in Minturn itself, which includes its own winery to slake the thirst of avid snow-lovers. Labels on the wines portray an old railway engine, and the label is a collectors' item in itself.

Bruce McLaughlin, who founded wineries in New Town, Connecticut and in Colorado Springs, founded Minturn Cellars in 1990. He taught the congenial Ted Dunn how to produce good spirits. There is a story that McLaughlin won a bet that he could make better wine than they made in California. Of course, no grapes are grown in Minturn's high altitude. Ted uses mostly Grand Valley products, but gets his Muscat grapes from Washington State.

There is a great charm in the building that houses the winery. It is in what was once a narrow alley, which brings to mind some of Europe's quaint urban and village wineries.

When driving into town from Interstate 70, take the first right and there you are, ready to be greeted by Ted. All the wine is marketed locally. Selections include Chardonnay, Merlot, Muscat Blanc, Cabernet, and, the most popular of all, Minturn Cellars' Riesling. There is a rustic tasting room, and cheese plates are available on the outdoor deck, where splendid views of towering peaks greet the eye.

The telephone number is 970-827-5918.

*The wall mural at the Rocky Hill winery will be moved in its entirety to
its new location near Grand Junction.*
Author Photo

ROCKY HILL WINERY

1997

COLORADO

COLORADO GROWN

PRODUCED AND BOTTLED BY ROCKY HILL WINERY
MONTROSE, CO ALCOHOL 12.1% BY VOLUME. CONTAINS SULFITES

As our label shows, the majestic San Juan
Mountains overlook the serene setting of
Montrose, Colorado. Located in the
Uncompahgre Valley, since 1881 Montrose has seen
cowboys, Ute Indians, gunfighters, farmers, sheep-
men, orchards, the 1909 Gunnison Tunnel, the Jack
Dempsey era, the Depression... to the city of today.
Now Montrose is home to Colorado's ninth
winery, owned by David Fansler. Visit the Rocky Hill
Winery and Tasting Room, located at 18380 S. Hwy
550, and sample our fine wines.

GOVERNMENT WARNING:
(1) ACCORDING TO THE SURGEON GENERAL, WOMEN SHOULD NOT
DRINK ALCOHOLIC BEVERAGES DURING PREGNANCY BECAUSE OF
THE RISK OF BIRTH DEFECTS. (2) CONSUMPTION OF ALCOHOLIC
BEVERAGES IMPAIRS YOUR ABILITY TO DRIVE A CAR OR OPERATE
MACHINERY, AND MAY CAUSE HEALTH PROBLEMS.

Where the Coyotes Stole the Grapes

ROCKY HILL WINERY
18380 Highway 550
Montrose 81401

*L*ocated just two miles south of Montrose on the highway to Ouray and Telluride, the Rocky Hill Winery finally had to fence its vineyard and strawberry patch because the coyotes and mule deer had discovered the tasty new offerings.

David Fansler moved from Pawnee, Illinois to Montrose in 1980. While he also is a playwright, his love with winemaking led him to the University of California at Davis (quite a few Colorado winemakers studied there) where he learned the art of winemaking well. He also took courses at Fresno State and Cornell University. In 1983 he planted his six-and-a-half acre roadside farm with grapevines. Unfortunately in 1995 David's plants suffered a major freeze-out, so he has since grown his grapes in the Grand Valley and makes trips several times a week to nurture them. He obtains the succulent cherries that are used in his popular wines from the Olathe area.

Rocky Hill produces a wide variety of wines. One of the most popular is made from tart pie cherries. Among the enticing blends are *Ski Bunny Blush, San Juan Gold, Wipe Out White, Black Canyon, Ouray,* and, of course, *Montrose. Howlin' Coyote Red* was the judges' favorite at the Southwest Wine Festival held at Ruidoso, New Mexico in 1994.

David and his wife, Marschall, hold forth at the winery tasting room on weekdays and Saturday afternoons during the summer and by appointment in the winter. A pleasant streamside picnic area provides views of the spectacular San Juan Mountains.

Rocky Hill wines are available all over Colorado and are the house wines at Brierhurst Manor in Manitou Springs. Plans are underway to move the winery to the Orchard Mesa region at Grand Junction. For now, the telephone number is 970-249-3765.

The fantastic view from Terror Creek Winery.
Author Photo

Terror Creek

1997

COLORADO

Pinot Noir

PRODUCED AND BOTTED BY TERROR CREEK WINERY
PAONIA, CO 81428 ALCOHOL 12% BY VOLUME CONTAINS SULFITES

Taking the name of the snow-fed stream tumbling along the property's edge, Terror Creek Winery enjoys a spectacular vista from atop 6400' high Garvin Mesa in the Rocky Mountains of Colorado. This pristine high altitude environment of hot sunny days, cool nights and low humidity, is ideal for the cultivation of premium grapes. Swiss-trained winemaker Joan Mathewson creates Alsatian-styled wines which are alive with fruit flavor and crisp acidity.

Way Up There on Terror Creek

TERROR CREEK WINERY
1750 4175 Road
Paonia 81428

hen a stream flowing down from the south flank of Grand Mesa went on a roaring rampage in the spring of 1883, settlers named it "Holy Terror Creek." Over the years, for some unexplained reason, it has been de-sanctified and no longer rates as "Holy."

High up on this stream, which flows into the North Fork of the Gunnison River near Paonia, is the vineyard of Terror Creek Winery. These are the highest commercial wine grapevines in the nation, and probably in North America, at 6,418 feet above sea level.

John Matthewson, a graduate of Colorado School of Mines, spent twenty-six years living outside the United States while engaged in oil exploration and cultivating a taste for fine wines. Joan Matthewson, a graduate of Colorado Women's College, studied in Switzerland, where she worked in vineyards and graduated as a winemaker from De Changin School. She is Colorado's only vintner with a European diploma.

The two met while skiing at Aspen, married, and sought a suitable site for growing grapes and making wines. Researchers from Colorado State University had determined that the upper reaches of Terror Creek could produce wine grapes if they were carefully tended.

Down-slope breezes flow through the North Fork Canyon almost every morning, and often up-slope zephyrs take over late in the day, helping to retard frost on these high grounds. Usually there is no killing frost until mid-October.

The canyonside has superb drainage since its soil is underlain by limestone. Watering is done from overhead sprinklers, so the vines receive the effect of rain. Joan maintains that this is more natural than either drip or flow water distribution.

The Terror Creek underground cellar is ideal for fermentation and aging. Their first bottling was in 1993. Terror Creek makes Chardonnay, Gewurztraminer, Riesling and Pinot Noir.

For directions to the winery, open weekend afternoons from Memorial Day to Labor Day, call 970-527-3484.

41

*Dianne Read at the aging barrels of
Cottonwood Cellars in Olathe, Colorado.
Author Photo*

Beneath the Spreading Cottonwoods

COTTONWOOD CELLARS, INC.
5482 Highway 348
Olathe 81425

*W*hen Diana and Keith Read bought a fifty-two-acre farm near Olathe, they intended to use it for vacations; but they soon gave up their California computer consulting careers to open a winery at the same spot in 1994. Keith, who obtained winemaking experience as he grew up in California, took on the responsibilities for production. His brother, Richard, took charge of the on-site vineyards, whose first vines were planted in 1995.

Located three-and-a-half miles west of the town of Olathe, beneath a cluster of huge cottonwood trees, the winery uses its own grapes; except for the Rieslings, which are brought in from Moab, Utah. In Olathe's productive farming region, nationally famous for the "Olathe Sweet" brand of sweet corn, people were shocked when the Reads scraped off the rich topsoil from their farm to expose the rocky subsoil that viniferous grapes prefer.

Diana and Keith have their own preferences, which center on heavy old-world red wines, including Lemberger, which are aged in French and American barrels. Their best-selling wines are the Cabernet Sauvignon and Carneros Chardonnay.

Sold all over Colorado, Cottonwood wines appear on the wine lists at Del Frisco's Eagle Steakhouse in Denver and the Black Bear at Green Mountain Falls. Their Reserve Merlot was featured in *Bon Appetit* magazine.

The tasting room hours at Cottonwood Cellars vary with the seasons. It is best to call before making the trip: 970-323-6224.

The attractive Mountain Spirit Winery.
  Photo Courtesy of Terry Barkett

Under the Angel of Shavano

MOUNTAIN SPIRIT WINERY
15750 County Road 220
Salida 81201

Every spring, usually sometime in June, the snows of 14,229-foot Mount Shavano, which towers over the town of Salida, start to melt. There then remains, for a short while, snow in some of the mountain's crevices, which form the shape of an angel. Many legends abound about the apparition. One tale tells of an Indian princess who prayed to her Gods after a dry season for more water. She ultimately sacrificed herself to the mountain; and as she melted, the waters came down to give new life to the valley below.

At the foot of this "angelic" peak is the Mountain Spirit Winery. Located about twelve miles west of Salida, the winery is situated on a five-acre homestead near what was once the town of Mayville.

Since 1995 Michael and Terry Barkett have created award-winning wines, many of which blend fruits and berries with grapes from the Grand Valley. At 8,000 feet above sea level, it may be the highest winery (as distinguished from vinery) in North America.

Terry has college degrees in Computer Science and Medical Technology. Michael is a surgeon who has written books on nutrition and food allergies. He is also president of the Colorado State Board of Health.

The old homestead house, in which the winery is located, usually features entertainment; and there are wine tastings on the old apple-loading dock in the summer. There are also frequent wildflower tours and, in the winter, snowshoe hikes.

Mountain Spirit wines may also be sampled at the tasting room in historic downtown Salida. The shop also includes art, jewelry, and angels created by local stylists and artists.

Perhaps the Mountain Spirit label makes the bottle a keepsake in itself. This exquisite work of art depicts a marvelous pink Native American angel and has been featured on the cover of *Wine Label* magazine. The label is the creation of Salida artist, Pat Oglesby.

Considering the various unique features of this establishment, there is certainly justification for the motto: "Quality Wines with a Difference."

Mountain Spirit Winery can be reached at 719-539-1175.

2000 Riesling

This sweet wine has a soft nose with sweet spice, flowers, Apricot & Apple aromas.

It is best served with a spicy dish or with pork or chicken. Enjoy!

WINEMAKER

PRODUCED AND BOTTLED BY
RONDON ENTERPRISES, INC.
CEDAREDGE, COLORADO
E-MAIL: smwine@stoneymesa.com
http://www.stoneymesa.com
(970) 856-7572

STONEY MESA

COLORADO

2000
Riesling

11.77% ALCOHOL BY VOLUME

At the Foot of Thunder Mountain

STONEY MESA WINERY
1619 2125 Drive
Cedaredge 81413

*I*t is believed that at one time the Ute Indian name for what is now called "Grand Mesa" was "Thunder Mountain." At the southern foot of the two-mile-high plateau nestles the charming town of Cedaredge. Nearby, at an elevation of 5,600 feet above sea level, are the vineyards of Stony Mesa Winery.

Donna and Ron Neal, originally hobby winemakers, planted their first vines in 1995. Despite some freeze-outs, they made their wine using their own grapes together with others from nearby Hotchkiss. Ron studied viticulture at the University of California, Davis. He and his son, Bret, make the wine.

They believe in aging their products for two to three years to enhance the flavor before storage. Their most popular wine is Gewurztraminer. They are also producing some mead, courtesy of the local honeybees, as well as other wines made from grapes.

Stony Mesa wines are available at most western Colorado liquor stores and are also marketed by Mountain Wine Distributing Company in Denver. They are also served at Tasso's Bistro in Georgetown and at the Spruce Lodge on Grand Mesa. Several tour groups make it a point to stop at the Stoney Mesa Winery for wine tastings. The winery also offers a summer concert series.

For a complete list of their wines or directions to the winery call 970-856-7572. Another Stoney Mesa tasting room, Red Mountain Ranches, is located at 1948 Highway 65 just north of Cedaredge, telephone 970-856-3803.

Old Town Arvada's Flour Mill. The Old Town Winery
is just around the corner.
Photo Courtesy of Nancy Lewis-Lentz

"Your Palate is my Canvas"

OLD TOWN WINERY
5659 Old Wadsworth Blvd.
Arvada 80002

*C*onrad Kindsfather, an Arvada attorney, recently purchased the Old Town Winery, which is located not far from the landmark flourmill that distinguishes that city's historic preservation area.

Randy Zeleny, a veteran of two decades of winemaking, originally founded the winery in 1997. His slogan was "Your palate is my canvas," and he practiced what he preached by making a fine art of his wines. Randy stated his philosophy as "Utilize and maximize the personality and potential of the grape at the time of the harvest with as little human intervention as possible." Kingsfather endorses and continues that philosophy of winemaking.

The Old Town Winery has won numerous awards, including "Best Overall Winery in Colorado" at the 1999 Snowmass Fall festival, and the "Peoples' Choice Award" at several Denver wine tastings. The company's barrel-fermented Chardonnay has been sold as a limited edition with that entire brand of wine's cases and bottles being numbered.

Kindsfather pointed out that Colorado Chardonnay grapes are superior to any other Chardonnay in the world. If this is indeed the case it lends some credibility to frequently heard stories that California and French winemakers are currently seeking to buy high-altitude land for use as Chardonnay vineyards in western Colorado.

A tasting can be available by appointment in the back part of a former store where the wine is made. Call the Old Town Winery at 888-990-WINE.

Customers enjoy the tasting room at Trail Ridge Winery.
Photo Courtesy of Trail Ridge Winery.

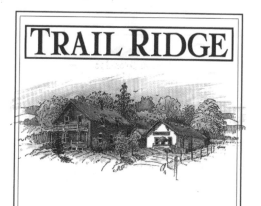

Lemberger in Loveland

TRAIL RIDGE WINERY
4113 Eisenhower Blvd. (U.S. Highway 34)
Loveland 80537

*E*xcept for those who live in or have visited the state of Washington, not many American wine-lovers have a chance to sample Lemberger. This wine, which originated in Germany, has a fruity, red, dry taste, which is very popular with its supporters. It is no longer exclusive to that state, since three Colorado wineries now make Lemberger. Trail Ridge Winery has won the gold medal for its Lemberger in international competition.

Tim Merrick, together with several partners, is the winemaker and owner of Trail Ridge. The farm is located beside the highway that goes up through Big Thompson Canyon and Rocky Mountain National Park, and eventually to Trail Ridge Road, which passes over the Continental Divide. It is the highest paved through-highway in the nation, although not open in the winter. The site of the winery is an old fruit farm that dates back to 1906.

A graduate of the University of Colorado, Tim spent some time in California learning the delights of good wines and in 1986 established North Denver Cellars to supply wine hobbyists with equipment and grapes. He opened the Trail Ridge Winery at Loveland in 1994, using local cherries for his wine. He now buys grapes from all over the state, including Cañon City and Olney Springs.

In addition to Lemberger, Trail Ridge has won medals for its Chardonnay and *Never Summer White,* named for a range of mountains not far away. *Prairie Rose* and *Fall River Red* are also special blends. Merlot is still the best-seller.

Ann Seewald, Colorado's respected pioneer winemaker and critic, considers Merrick to be one of the best wine making practitioners in Colorado.

The tasting room is open every day in the summer, and afternoons in spring and autumn. Telephone 970-635-0949.

The Canyon Wind Cellars at Palisade, Colorado.
Author Photo

The vineyard at Canyon Wind Cellars.
Author Photo

Why Pepi Came to Palisade

CANYON WIND CELLARS
3904 North River Road
Palisade 81526

Norman and Ellen Christianson loved wine and decided to start a winery. They toured the West Coast of the United States, as well as Australia, South Africa, and Chile in their quest for the best grapes. Norman was a geologist from Douglas County, Colorado. They were delighted to eventually find that the optimal combination of best growing conditions occurred just across the mountains, along the Colorado River across from Palisade — the historic Vineland area. At the time of the Christiansons search it was noted for its tasty fruits, and the Vineland had grown very few grapes since Prohibition times.

Establishing the Canyon Wind Cellars, the Christiansons planted twenty-four acres of vines in 1991. Then they talked one of California's renowned Napa Valley winemakers, Robert Pepi, into coming to Colorado. He designed the winery and produced the original wine. It was Pepi who left his mark on the whole operation: long-term aging in oak, blends made with the best fruits, and the winery itself, which now has underground cellars.

Pepi passed his art on to Cameron Lyeth (pronounced "Leeth"). Cameron had been cellar master for three years for Arrowood Winery in California. He has since left Canyon Wind to establish Garfield Estates Winery.

In 1996 the first wines from the estate-grown grapes were produced. The Merlot and Cabernet Sauvignon both won medals at the Los Angeles County Fair, one of the most competitive tastings in the nation.

Wine expert Michael Lonsford, of the *Houston Chronicle,* declared Canyon Wind's *1999 Chardonnay* the best in the nation.

A British winemaker, Ben Parsons, has recently taken over production. Ben has a degree in oenology (viticulture) from the University of Adelaide in Australia.

Canyon Wind wines are marketed in Texas, Illinois, Tennessee, New Hampshire, and North Carolina, as well as in Colorado. The tasting room is open weekdays and Saturdays. There is also a picnic area on the attractive grounds. Telephone 970-464-0888.

The entry to Rocky Mountain Meadery.

Author Photo

Confre Cellars and Rocky Mountain Meadery Tasting Room.
Author Photo

Mellow Meads and Sparkling Ciders

CONFRE CELLARS

Rocky Mountain Meadery & Rocky Mountain Cidery
3701 G Road
Palisade 81526

*M*ead, which is made from honey, is the oldest form of wine known. Its use goes back perhaps 10,000 years, and reference to it was found in the hieroglyphics of the earliest Egyptian pyramids. The ancient Greeks found out about mead and rejoiced in it, the Romans loved it, the Vikings considered it the "wine of the gods," and in the Middle Ages, the English named it "mead", a derivation of the original Greek word "met." They called it wine fit for kings.

"Meadery" and "cidery" are not in the dictionary, as they are words coined by Fred and Connie Strothman and copyrighted by them.

Fred, who also makes grape wines for St. Kathryn Cellars, considers honey wine the most difficult and demanding to produce. The honey comes from California and is made by bees that feed on orange blossoms rather than Colorado alfalfa. One might think all honey wine would be sweet, but that is not the case. Mead ranges from *King Arthur,* very dry, through *Lancelot* and *Guinevere* to sweet *Camelot* and fruit blends. Incidentally, the word "honeymoon" came from the custom of giving newlyweds a couple of months' supply of mead to ensure that the marriage would be fruitful and soon produce offspring.

The cidery operation, known as "Pinnacle Gold Ciders," makes alcoholic ciders from apples and pears.

Fred was a judge in Denver for eighteen years. After he and Connie bought a farm at Palisade for semi-retirement, they became very interested in making wine. The founder of the Colorado wine industry, Jim Seewald, helped Fred cultivate the necessary skills to establish the meadery. There has been no retirement since then, but the Strothmans love the artistry of making unique products.

Meadery wines are featured at the Larkspur and other Renaissance Festivals, and at the Excalibur hotel and casino at Las Vegas.

The tasting room is open daily except for major holidays. Telephone 970-464-7899 or 800-720-2558.

Meadery wines are also sampled and purchased at Honeyville, ten miles north of Durango and at the Durango Mall. Call 800-676-7690.

Bill and Anita Donahue, proud owners of Creekside Cellars.
Photo Courtesy of Joseph D. Shields

The tasting bar at Creekside Cellars. Photo Courtesy of Joseph D. Shields

This Makes Good Scents

CREEKSIDE CELLARS
28036 Highway 74
Evergreen 80439

Bill Donahue started making fruit wines in 1980. He and his wife, Anita, whose forebears are true Italians, obtained a wine license in 1996 and began to also produce grape wines at their winery in Evergreen, Colorado in 2000. Their grapes are all obtained from contract growers near Palisade in the Grand Valley viticultural area.

While Chardonnay is the most popular wine at Creekside Cellars, they also make Merlot, Pinot Noir, and Sauvignon Blanc. They specialize in Lake Haus Port and Black Muscat Port.

One of the principal attractions to their winery is its delicatessen. "Customers come here just for the smell of it," Biil reports. The fragrant smells of wines such as Port, a good selection of cheeses, and many Italian meats makes visiting their winery a gourmet experience. The dining room overlooks nearby Bear Creek. Curious deer and elk often peek in at the guests, who include a regular group of wine enthusiasts who come to socialize at Creekside Cellars.

Creekside Cellars is a very popular tourist stop and also daily attracts many Denver wine lovers who escape from the city in the summer to enjoy the cool, shady mountains at Evergreen, often spending the entire afternoon on the deck above the creek.

All of Creekside wines are sold at their establishment. They state "At Creekside we celebrate the relationship of good food and good wine shared with family and friends. Thank you for making our wine a part of your every day celebrations of life."

Call 303-674-5460 to obtain the seasonal hours for tasting.

By Lydia Maurer, Gunnison

Vins de Garage

ASPEN VALLEY WINERY
197 Coyote Circle
Carbondale 81623

*S*omething of a revolution has occurred recently in the Bordeaux region of France. The movement is called *vins de garage* or "garage wineries." It seems that a few individualists have been making superb wines in their garages, and some have even won the top ratings in Paris wine tasting contests, beating out the famous wineries of France!

Colorado also has its own premier garage winery, located in the Blue Lake area of Carbondale. Patrick and Katie Leto market their wine products at the Aspen Farmers' Mart from June through October each year; and yes, the fermentation and aging of the wines are carried on in the garage of their home.

It all started when Patrick and another Italian friend decided that all young men of that descent should be able to make their own wines, according to the tradition handed down over the years by their ancestors.

In 1996, they entered a bottle of their Merlot in the Colorado State Fair using a crayon-drawn label by Patrick and Katie's seven-year-old daughter, Alicia. Their entry won the award of the "best amateur wine." When a local newspaper wrote up the story, the Associated Press picked it up, and their fame spread throughout the United States.

Since then, the partner has dropped out of the business; but encouragement from friends led to the founding of the winery by the Letos.

Using a variety of grapes from Palisade, Aspen Valley has added Chardonnay and Cabernet Franc, as well as a blend of the latter, and Merlot. Their telephone number is 970-704-WINE.

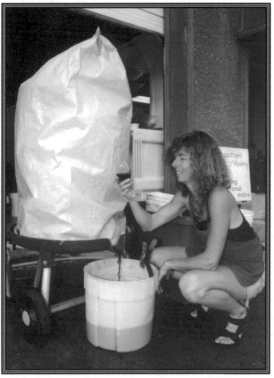

Marianne "Gussie" Walter of Augustina's Winery.
Photo Courtesy of Charlie Fellenbaum

Gussie's One-Woman Winery

AUGUSTINA'S WINERY
4715 N. Broadway, B-3
Boulder 80304

*M*arianne Walter, who also goes by the name of "Gussie," runs the only one-woman winery in the state of Colorado and, perhaps, in the nation. While she drafts her father into service to help with picking and transporting of the grapes across the Continental Divide during the brief harvest season, she is solely responsible for making the wine products and the winery sales. She is the imaginative blender of such award-winning wines as *Wine Chick Red* and *Wine Chick White*.

Marianne is a former geologist who "dropped out of polite society" in 1997 to crush and ferment her own special vintages.

Gussie's output is available mostly in Boulder and Denver stores but also in some of the "funkier restaurants" in the area as well as at the winery itself.

Her colorful and creative labels have won awards; but even if you're not tasting her wine, take a look at her unique labels for an art experience.

While the quality of Gussie's wine is up to the distinctive Colorado standards, her prices are competitive with some mass-produced wine imported from other states and countries.

Try *Wine Chick White, Blue, Rosé,* or *Red;* the popular *Harvest Gold;* smoky-herbal *Ruby;* or *Joi de Vino Chardonnay,* — "a wine to go with old novels...Thomas Hardy if you are feeling serious...Jane Austen if you are not."

Call ahead for tasting room hours: 303-549-2047.

The entry to the tasting room of DeBeque Canyon Winery.
Author Photo

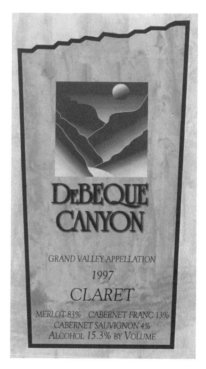

A Real Pioneer

DEBEQUE CANYON WINERY
3943 Highway 6
Palisade 81526

*B*ennett Price was one of the original investors in Jim Seewald's pioneering Colorado Mountain Vineyards back in 1977. He learned to make wine under the tutelage of Seewald and the celebrated wine making expert, Erik Bruner.

Bennett has personally planted about seventy-five percent of the vineyards in the Grand Valley. He is a former president of the Rocky Mountain Association of Vintners and Viticulturalists.

He and his wife Davelyn ("Davy") bought their own vineyard in 1982 and then moved to the Grand Valley in 1986, where they worked and spent time improving several of the early Grand Valley vineyards. Their own winery was licensed by 1997.

The Prices opened a tasting room near the left bank of the Colorado River close to Palisade in August 2001. Farmers had been growing Zinfandel and Muscat grapes near the mouth of Rapid Creek as early as 1919; the vines being protected from frosts by the heat radiation effect of nearby Mount Lincoln and the breezes of DeBeque Canyon.

Bennett and Davy believe in the long-term barrel aging of wine. They use barrels of both American and French oak brought in from California. Among their selections are Pinot Noir, Cabernet Sauvignon, Viognier, and Syrah. A special blend is Claret, an old English term for red Bordeaux wine combinations. Merlot is their most popular product.

DeBeque Canyon wines are available at most Grand Valley liquor stores and are also the house wines at the popular restaurant, Mama Longo's, in Grand Junction. The Debeque Canyon tasting room, converted from what was once a fruit stand, is open on Fridays, Saturdays, and Sundays. Call 970-464-0559 for more information.

Fine grapes from the Grande River vineyards are used in Steamboat Springs Cellars wine.

Author Photo

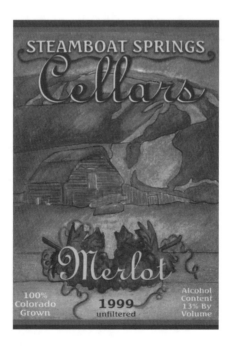

Wallpaper Hangers Make Good Wine

STEAMBOAT SPRINGS CELLARS
W-8 Yampa Valley Business Park
2464 Downhill Drive
Steamboat Springs 80487

*U*p in north-central Colorado in Steamboat Springs (Colorado's original "Ski Country U.S.A.") Tom Williams makes a living as a skillful paperhanger. His wife, Kathie, also hangs wallpaper, is a dog-sitter, and free-lances at other jobs.

According to Tom, he and Kathie loved good dry wines but were "too cheap" to buy what they wanted, so they decided to make their own wine from grapes grown at the Grande River Vineyards in Palisade. They believe that the Western Slope's warm days and cool nights produce Colorado's finest wine grapes. Tom and Kathie marketed their first bottles of Merlot, 225 cases in all, and found that many others had their same demanding tastes. They sold out their entire inventory the very first year. Now they are producing 750 to 800 cases a year and testing markets in Denver, Boulder, and Grand Junction.

The Williams have added Chardonnay, Sauvignon Blanc, Cabernet Blanc (called *Rabbit Ears* after the nearby mountain), and *Strawberry Park* (named for another locally famous site), which blend includes California strawberries.

Local artist Betsy Whitmore designed their colorful label. A side panel reads: "Although our facility is cramped with racks of oak barrels, we would love for you to come out and talk wine. But when you do, please call ahead so we'll have some wine ready." The number to call is 970-879-7501.

Crushed by Friends

SURFACE CREEK WINERY
2071 N. Road
Eckert 81418

W hen it comes time for the fall grape harvest, nearby friends and neighbors congregate at the Surface Creek vineyards in Delta County. There they help Jim and Jeanne Durr pick and then crush their grapes, and they usually bring along a supply of home-brewed beer. When the job is finished, there is a big harvest dinner.

Surface Creek Winery produces about 900 cases of wine each year, using its own grapes as well as grapes grown near Moab, Utah. Jim's wines include Merlot, Sauvignon Blanc, Chenin Blanc, and Cherry. Surface Creek wines have won awards in Colorado winefests.

Originally a lawyer, Jim recently retired as a wildlife biologist at Fort Collins. When he and Jeanne bought a farm in the lush Surface Creek Valley, friend Ron Neal, who founded the Stoney Creek Winery at nearby Cedaredge, encouraged them to plant grapes on two acres of their land. They opened the winery in 1998.

Jeanne manages the gift shop at the winery. The Durrs are enjoying winemaking, citing the congenial relations and camaraderie with others in the wine-making field, as well as the enthusiasm of their wine-loving customers.

The winery, tasting room, and gift shop are located a half mile west of the landmark stone church in the center of Eckert. Tastings are invited from 11 to 5 in the summer. Telephone them at 970-835-9463 (WINE).

The French country chateau style of the Two Rivers Winery tasting room.
Author Photo

The Look and Taste of Old France

TWO RIVERS WINERY
(CHATEAU DEUX FLEUVES)
2087 Broadway
Grand Junction 81503

*W*hen you view the beautiful vineyards and the country chateau, you might have the illusion you are in French wine country, except that the backdrop for the scene consists of the spectacular cliffs of Colorado National Monument. Two Rivers Winery, named for the nearby junction of the Colorado and Gunnison Rivers, is located in the Redlands region of Grand Junction, in an area that had been the site of viniferous grape-growing a century ago; but Two Rivers is the first licensed winery to be located there.

It was created by Bob and Billie Witham. Bob was a native of Craig, and Billie a native of Meeker. After a successful career of developing assisted-living communities, they retired from Austin, Texas, to explore western Colorado. As dedicated wine enthusiasts, they settled on the Redlands, planting eleven acres of grapes in 1999. Then they found Glen Foster, who had a science and teaching background and eight years of successful winemaking. As their winemaker, he has used the most modern equipment and has produced award-winning Riesling, Merlot, Chardonnay, and Cabernet Sauvignon.

The winery itself is called Chateau Deux Fleuves, meaning "house on two rivers." It is a graceful structure in the center of the vineyard. Since it was built, the Withams have added a matching 13,000 square-foot events center with nine bed and breakfast guest rooms upstairs. The main floor seats up to 150 people, and there are smaller meeting rooms.

Inside the winery itself are the fermentation tanks, barrel room, and tasting room. Murals depicting French village life lend a special charm to the various chambers. A cozy fireplace warms visitors on the rare inclement days.

Two Rivers wines are sold in many Colorado cities and towns. They are already on the wine lists of quite a few upscale restaurants. The tasting room and gift shop are open seven days a week, 10:30 AM - 6:00 PM Monday through Saturday; noon until 5:00 PM on Sundays.

If in doubt about how to reach this unique destination vineyard and winery, call 970-255-1471.

The Book Cliff Vineyards are located far away from the Boulder winery.
Photo Courtesy of Christopher Brown

From the BookCliffs to the Flatirons

BOOKCLIFF VINEYARDS
5501 Aztec Court
Boulder 80303

In the evening shadows of the Flatirons, Ulla Merz and John Garlich have created an unusual winery in the cellar of their Boulder home. John is the winemaker, but both he and Ulla spend their weekends tending their grapes near Palisade, at the foot of the Bookcliff Mountains. They use some of their grapes themselves; they sell the rest to other vintners.

It was in the 1970s that John dug a wine cellar in the basement and planted grapes in the backyard. John produced a Zinfandel in 1983 from California grapes. The couple discovered the Grand Valley in 1994 and bought a ten-acre peach orchard, gradually turning it into a vineyard growing Chardonnay, Cabernet, Sauvignon, Merlot, Viognier, and Cabernet Franc grapes.

Both Ulla and John are engineers. She is a software engineer; he is a civil engineer. They drive over to Palisade on Friday evenings during the growing season and toil among the vines, spending the nights in their trailer. Then they must wait until late Sunday for the return trip to avoid the bumper-to-bumper traffic returning home on I-70.

In 1999 their winery was licensed, but not without some trouble from an inspector who had never encountered a basement operation. After checking, he found that a number of wineries in California and New Mexico were located in approved cellars.

Ulla says that growing grapes and making wine from those grapes "has an aura of romance around it." This tender-loving care is one element that gives Colorado's winemakers such superior products.

BookCliff Cellars does not maintain a tasting room, but the wine is sold at the Boulder Farmers' Market on Saturdays from April to October.

The telephone number for BookCliff Cellars is 303-499-7301.

71

I.A. Balistreri Vineyard wine compliments
a wonderful gift basket.
Photo Courtesy of Bob C. Dougherty, Palisade Tribune

From Carnations to Chardonnay

J.A. BALISTRERI VINEYARDS
1946 E. 66th Avenue
Denver 80229

A half century ago the City of Denver was the major supplier of fresh Colorado carnations. There were several large greenhouses sending the distinctive blooms to florists far and wide. One of these greenhouses still grows flowers, but now its main product is wine.

John Balistreri makes his wine from four acres of grapes that are grown by his brother-in-law, Clyde Spero. John's uncles started making Muscat wines at their home in 1991. By 1998 the Balistreri commercial winery was licensed by the State of Colorado.

Much of the wine is made from grapes grown on his property, which is a former farm. The Balistreri underground drip system is used to carry compressed air during the winter, in order to keep the soil warm; and, when necessary, the vines are covered for protection.

Balistreri prides himself on his "all natural" wines, fermented one barrel at a time, using neither added yeast nor sulphides. He has also used some grapes in his wine from other parts of Colorado and California, as well as Colorado cherries.

Among his products are Chardonnay, Merlot, Cabernet Sauvignon, Syrah, Muscat, and Semillon. Fresh flowers and gift baskets are available at the winery, which is open on Saturday afternoons and by appointment. Wine and cheese parties may also be arranged. Call 303-287-5156.

Dan and Eva Baharav, owners of Baharav Vineyards.
Author Photo

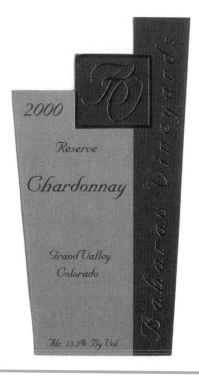

Ecological Refinement

BAHARAV VINEYARDS
2370 Road 112
Carbondale 81623

Dan and Eva Baharav were both born in Israel. They met in Aspen and fell in love with each other and with Western Colorado.

Dan was reared in a farming area and became a Professor of Ecology at the Israel Institute of Technology. Realizing the ideal all-around growing conditions for grapes in the East Orchard Mesa region near Palisade, the Baharavs purchased twelve acres and set out grape vines in 1995. Dan claims, "The Grand Valley is the best place in the universe to grow wine grapes." Their vineyard is not merely organic; it is a model of ecologically sensitive agriculture — a harmony of soil, water, climate, and personal husbandry. Even the birds that come to pluck the grapes shrink away when they hear the recorded sounds of raptors nearby.

Eva is a scholar of ancient Jewish wine growing. The Hebrew word for sulfur comes from the practice of "throwing powdered rocks" on the leaves of vines to protect them from mildew.

The winery is located in a secluded forest area not far from the town of Carbondale at 7,000 feet above sea level. Baharav's vineyards, located about 2,000 feet lower in elevation, get careful attention. If occasional rains fall in the summer, Dan drives down early the next day to pull the wet leaves back from the fruit, which must not be shaded from the sun. No organic compounds are used in the carefully groomed vineyard — yet only grass may grow around the delicate roots.

In 1998 Eva and Dan were able to make their first wines: Chardonnay, Cabernet Franc/Merlot, Merlot, Viognier, Syrah and Muscat. Only about six hundred cases a year are produced. The vintners like to go light on oak aging to prevent alteration of the pure flavors. The dry wines are unfiltered to preserve the taste.

In addition to marketing in the Glenwood Springs-Aspen area, Baharav Vineyard wines are available at the Boulder Liquor Mart and at the upscale Aubergnine Cafe in downtown Denver.

As Dan and Eva personally care for every detail from vine to bottle, theirs is a designated Estate Winery in the Grand Valley Viticultural Area.

The telephone number to call is 877-ECO-WINE.

The wine flows freely at the Palisade Wine Festival.
Photo Courtesy of Bob C. Dougherty, Palisade Tribune

A Hidden Treasure in McElmo Canyon

SUTCLIFFE VINEYARDS
12202 Road G
Cortez 81325

*J*ohn Sutcliffe moved from his home in Great Britain to New York City in 1968, and he established a successful restaurant there. Later he became a restaurateur in the southern United States, where he cultivated a gourmet's appreciation of fine wines and the fine art of wine making.

McElmo Canyon is located in the southwest corner of Colorado. It is renowned as the home of prehistoric ancient Indian cultures (primarily the Anasazi, now known as the Ancestral Puebloians) who built their "cities" in that vicinity. The canyon stretches all the way from Cortez to the Utah border.

The farm where John and his wife, Emily, a Cortez physician, raise hay and cattle (and now wine) is located about fifteen miles into McElmo Canyon. Formerly John had a ranch near Carbondale, Colorado. In 1997 the Sutcliffes started a small winery, growing their own grapes in the sheltering canyon, which has a remarkably warm climate. The Anasazi had good reason for living there!

Merlot is the wine that is the most in demand from the Sutcliffe Vineyards, but Cabernet Franc and Syrah are also produced. There is no marketing as such, as the entire production of Sutcliffe Vineyards (about 350 barrels) is usually sold out in advance to people who come and pick up the wine after it has properly aged.

The Sutcliffe's telephone number is 970-565-0825.

St. Kathryn Cellars Winery and Tasting Room. Author Photo

Patrons enjoy St. Kathryn Cellars' wine tasting room in Palisade, Colorado. Author Photo

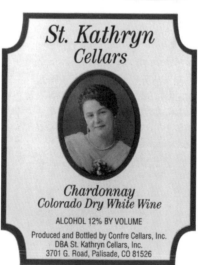

St. Kathryn Cellars

Chardonnay
Colorado Dry White Wine

ALCOHOL 12% BY VOLUME

Produced and Bottled by Confre Cellars, Inc.
DBA St. Kathryn Cellars, Inc.
3701 G. Road, Palisade, CO 81526

Cranberry Kiss and Blueberry Bliss

ST. KATHRYN CELLARS
785 Elberta Avenue
Palisade 81526

S t. Kathryn Cellars' wines are made from grapes grown on East Orchard Mesa and also from Palisade fruits.

Fred Strothman (an ex-judge) is the St. Kathryn's winemaker, and the winery got its title from the name of his mother. Kathryn Strothman promised, before she passed away, "to keep an eye on the vineyard" when in heaven. Their wine reflects their commitment to honor her. The wines that they make include four different Chardonnays, four Merlots, and three blends, in addition to the "Colorado Country Wines."

Colorado Country Wines are fruit wines, advertised as wines "like Grandma used to make" perhaps a century ago. They include *Cranberry Kiss, Apple Blossom, Golden Pear,* and St. Kathryn's signature wine, *Blueberry Bliss.*

St. Kathryn Cellars opened in August of 1999. The tasting room includes "fine wines, gourmet foods, gifts and a warm welcome from your hosts." The winery also includes a catering facility and grounds that were specifically designed for weddings, business meetings and other special occasions. Mt. Garfield and Grand Mesa provide spectacular views from the winery, while you are sampling their fine wines.

Jane Foster presides over the large tasting room and gift shop, located just off Exit 42 on Interstate 70 at Palisade. There is also an indoor catering and events center which can accommodate up to 200 people. Telephone 970-464-9288.

*Gene and
Lorinda Corley
of Corley
Vineyards.
Author Photo*

*This old wine press (above) at
Corley Vineyards
contrasts sharply with the
new ones (right).*

Author Photo

Old Wine in New Bottles

CORLEY VINEYARDS
2830 G.25 Road
Palisade 81526

There is a Biblical admonition not to put new wine in old bottles. Never fear! At Corley Vineyards the wines are barrel-aged longer than almost anywhere else to bring forth their "big, full-bodied" wines.

In 1997 winemaker Gene Corley and his wife Lorinda, spent their fifteenth wedding anniversary in Santa Barbara, California, where they met and were given a tour by the famous winemaker, Fess Parker. This was the inspiration for the Coloradans from Morrison to learn how to make wines that are comparable to California's best.

They sold their demanding ATM-security-armored-car business that stretched over six states and employed hundreds of workers; and the Corleys purchased a barren six-acre plot in 1999 that had formerly been a peach orchard. They planted their viniferous grapes and crushed grapes from California while waiting for their own vines to produce.

In 2001 they were able to make wine from their own estate vineyards: Chardonnay, Cabernet Sauvignon, Merlot, and later, Syrah and Muscat. Their drip irrigation system flows through the vineyards' well-drained and sandy soils into the river, a good stone's throw away from the vineyard.

Gene and Lorinda intend to keep their winery small, producing only 2,500 cases a season, or between five- and six-thousand gallons of wine. While their two sons help out from time to time, the Corleys do most of the work themselves and no longer have to manage a huge number of employees, as they had in their former business.

Their wine is aged a long time in kegs made from Missouri oak. It is then poured into new bottles and the attractive peacock labels, which Lorinda designed, are attached.

Gene's grandfather made wine in Italy a century ago. He brought to America the aged wine press that he used in that country, which is on display at Corley Vineyards. It can squeeze out about two gallons with each pressing. Telephone 970-464-5314 for more information.

The Newcomers

Fine wine ages at Puesta Del Sol Winery.
Photo Courtesy of Eames Peterson

A New Paonia Winery on the Sunset Slope

PUESTA DEL SOL WINERY
1189 4050 Road
Paonia 81428

One of Colorado's newest wineries is located near Paonia, in the North Fork of the Gunnison River Valley. Puesta Del Sol began production in December 2001. The name of the winery means "Sunset" in Spanish. Paonia is located on the "sunset slope" or Western Slope of the Rocky Mountains, hence the name Puesta Del Sol Winery.

Eames and Pamela Petersen have set out three-and-a-half acres of grape vines and are now producing Pinot Noir, with future plans for some other very special wines. They are self-marketing their product to various outlets in the area but do not have a tasting room at present and accept visitors by appointment only.

For further information, call 970-527-6296.

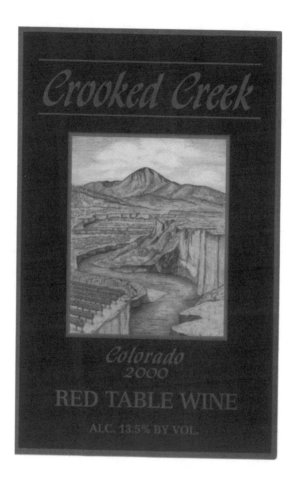

Vast Vineyards and Strawbale Structures

GUY DREW VINEYARDS
Crooked Creek Cellars
20057 Road G
Cortez 81321

In 1997 Guy and Ruth Drew left their corporate careers on the Front Range of Colorado to establish a large vineyard and winery that will eventually produce about 7,000 cases a year. The result was the second winery to be located in McElmo Canyon near Cortez.

Within view of Mesa Verde and Sleeping Ute Mountain, they developed a 194-acre farm and set a goal to plant 36,000 vines in four years using only a part of their total acreage. By late 2001 their earliest bottling of red and white table wines had been accomplished.

The strawbale home, bunkhouse, guesthouse, and large winery are now a reality, as well as the producing grapevines. California vineyard consultant, Richard Nagaoka, helped the Drews with the preparation of their land, trellising, and the installation of the drip irrigation systems.

When plowing the land, they turned up an archaeological ruin in the center of the proposed vineyard. Such sites should not be disturbed, so the Drews then contracted with another farmer to plant 7,000 vines on his property in order to stay on the planting schedule. Thus a total of 18,000 vines were planted on the Drew's "site-free" area and the borrowed field in six days.

The plantings were for Cabernet Sauvignon, Cabernet Franc, Merlot, Syrah, Chardonnay, and Sauvignon Blanc. In the meantime, they have been purchasing grapes from the Grand Valley and from Moab, Utah.

In the near future Guy and Ruth should have eleven varieties of wine produced from their own grapes. Guy was appointed to the Colorado Wine Industry Development Board in 2001.

The telephone number for Guy Drew Vineyards is 970-565-4958.

The Reeder Mesa Vineyard near Whitewater, Colorado.
Photo Courtesy of Douglas Vogal

2001
Colorado
White Riesling

VINTED AND BOTTLED BY
REEDER MESA VINEYARDS
WHITEWATER, COLORADO
ALCOHOL 13.7% BY VOLUME
BW-CO-47   CONTAINS SULFITES

Reeder Mesa Vineyards is situated in the foothills of the world's largest flat-top mountain, the Grand Mesa, at an elevation of 5600 feet.

The first white riesling grapes were planted in 1994, and after receiving numerous winemaking awards at the amateur level, Reeder Mesa Vineyards was established in 2000.

We hope you enjoy this vintage!

Serve chilled with hors d'oeuvres, or as an accompaniment to fish, poultry, pork, or your favorite dessert.

Ordering Information
Fax: 970-255-7393

Where the Elk Get Together

REEDER MESA VINEYARDS
7799 Reeder Mesa Road
Whitewater 81527

*L*ocated eight miles east of Whitewater, between Grand Junction and Delta, Reeder Mesa is situated at 5,600 feet above sea level, and is overlooked by the west face of Grand Mesa, which rises almost a mile higher in elevation. As the late autumn snows come, the elk herds descend on the vineyards. Douglas Vogel, winemaker, and his wife, Kristen, have had to erect a high fence to protect their vines, yet at least a hundred of the wapiti set up winter camp outside the vineyard, foraging on other goodies and evidently hoping the fence will fall!

The first acre of Riesling grapes was planted in 1994, and two more acres were set out in the former cattle ranch in 2000.

The Vogels bottled their initial offering, a hundred cases of vintage 2000 Riesling, in 2001. There are plans to also make Merlot in the future years.

While Reeder Mesa Vineyards has no tasting room at present, those wondering how to reach the vineyards may contact the Vogels at 970-242-7468.

The winery at Garfield Estates Winery.
Author Photo

Cameron Lyeth, winemaker at
Garfield Estates Vineyards.
Author Photo

How About Some Fumé Blanc?

GARFIELD ESTATES WINERY
3572 G Road
Palisade 81526

There is a dry, white variation of Sauvignon Blanc known as Fumé Blanc — pronounced "Foomay Blahn." It is named for the French word for "smoke" and suggests such a flavor and scent. This is the premier offering of one of the newest wineries in the Palisade region. The winery itself is a beautiful remodeling of an 80-year old barn.

Garfield Estates Winery states that it is focused on producing "the finest wine from premium Western Colorado grapes." They intend (in fact they say they insist) on low yields from the vineyard and give special attention to the details in their wine cellar. The distinctive weathervane used on their label is actually situated at the top of their winery.

Former Canyon Winds winemaker, Cameron Lyeth, joined Jeff Carr and Dave McLoughlin to develop the attractive Garfield Estates Winery, named for the mountain which overlooks their eleven acres of vineyards. Garfield Estates' Rosé and Merlot are also available in the on-site tasting room.

Jeff lives in Boulder and Dave lives in Denver. Cameron, who directs the operation, comes from a family of winemakers. His father had a winery in Sonoma, California.

For their current status, you can call Cameron at 970-464-0941.

Graystone Vineyards with Mt. Garfield in the background.
Author Photo

Unique Boutique Winemaker

GRAYSTONE VINEYARDS
3334 F Road
Clifton 81520

Barbara and Robert Maurer returned to their native soil near Palisade following retirement from careers in Anchorage, Alaska. Robert is a dentist, and Barbara has a law degree.

Now the Maurers are just reaping the harvest of their Graystone Vineyards and producing dry, slightly gray Pinot Gris, white Pino Blanc and heady red Port — all boutique products. Barbara serves as the winemaker. They make only a limited amount of these carefully developed wines.

The gray face of Mount Garfield, which overlooks the winery, gave the name to the vineyards. The winery is located just east of downtown Clifton.

To sip these unique wines, which are available by appointment only, call 970-523-5132.

REDSTONE
MEADERY

Black Raspberry Nectar
Honey Wine with Black Raspberry Puree

Produced and Packed by Redstone Meadery
4700 Pearl Street Unit 2-A Boulder CO 80301
8% Alcohol by Volume 1/2 Gallon

"Nectar of the Gods" in Boulder

REDSTONE MEADERY
4700 Pearl Street
Boulder 80301

avid Myers and Julia Herz first offered their honey wine in June of 2001. Those flavors were *Black Raspberry* and *Boysenberry Nectar.*

Named for the Flatirons formation overlooking Boulder, Julia claimed that their winery is the first and only place in the nation serving draft mead, a sparkling nectar which is eight percent alcohol. There were plans to introduce *Mountain Honey,* twelve percent, during 2002.

Using honey from Lyons, Redstone has plans for many other fruity combinations. Mead was considered the legendary "nectar of the gods" and was noted in English literature as early as the eighth century. In fact, one may also purchase copies of Beowulf, the first epic poem, in the tasting room. Tasting is available Wednesday through Saturday afternoons. Tours are also conducted by request.

Ms. Herz also suggested that there may be a potential tasting room at the charming mountain town named Redstone, south of Carbondale. Telephone 720-406-1215.

Jim Griffin and his dog, Avanti, for whom the winery is named.
Photo Courtesy of Joseph D. Shields

Griff Goes Forward

AVANTI WINERY
9046 West Bowles Avenue
Littleton 80123

*J*im "Griff" Griffin has a loyal dog named Avanti, French for "Go Forward!" or "Onward!" One day when Griff was exhausted by the tribulations of making an application for a Colorado winery license, he became very discouraged. Then he glanced out the window and saw Avanti wagging his tail in encouragement. Jim kept on trying and was able to get his license in May of 2001, so the winery is actually named after "man's best friend."

Jim Griffin is a great supporter of all Colorado wines, and he sells fourteen other different winery's brands while waiting for his own label to come of age. His wines will include a limited edition Port, *Avanti Merlot,* and *Avanti Chardonnay.*

Those people who appreciate good smokes may want to visit the walk-in humidor in his tasting room for their choice of cigars and pipe tobacco, so Jim named his tasting room " 'Gars and Grapes." Jim will also tell you the latest information available on most of the other Colorado wineries.

If you want to know how to get there, call 303-904-7650.

Stomping grapes the old-fashioned way at the Palisade Wine Festival.

Photo Courtesy of Bob C. Dougherty,
Palisade Tribune

Vino e Buono!: Wine is Good!

SPERO WINERY
6579 Xavier Street
Arvada 80003

C lyde Spero's father emigrated from Potenza, Italy, as a child of thirteen years. He had already learned from his father how to make the traditional wines of Potenza, and he then passed the art on to his own son, Clyde. Clyde's wife, June, is the sister of John Balistreri, who operates the J.A. Balistreri Winery in Denver.

Spero Winery was licensed in 1997. It uses grapes from the Balistreri-Spero Vineyards in Adams County, planted in 1977, as well as grapes from the Grand Valley of Colorado and from Lodi, California. Their specialties are the red wines, but the Speros also offer Muscat, the traditional white made by the Italian-American community in Colorado.

While there is no tasting room at the time of this writing, it is expected one will open soon at the winery, which will be located on West 64th Street. (the Xavier address is the Spero's home.) The wines will be sold under the name *Vino e Buono,* Italian for "Wine is Good."

Call 303-831-3358 daytime, or 303-428-9830 (home).

The Holy Cross Abbey at Cañon City is a beautiful structure.
Drawing Courtesy of Holy Cross Abbey

In the Offing

HOLY CROSS ABBEY
Cañon City 81212

*T*he monastery at the beautiful Holy Cross Abbey in Cañon City was in trouble. There was not enough money to keep up the large grounds, and if something wasn't done soon the abbey would have to close. So the monks thought of several options. One was to sell the land and move elsewhere. Another was to sell a part of the land for development.

After considerable thought and prayer, the monks came up with an even better idea — a vineyard and a winery. It would allow the grounds to retain their secluded and pastoral look (even though Cañon City is developing all around it); and it would also bring in the necessary income that the monks needed to keep the abbey open.

At this time about 650 Chardonnay vines have been planted. Reverend Gregory Legge reports that plans call for about ten acres of vineyards in Cañon City and twenty more acres of vineyards at an abbey-owned ranch near the town of Wetmore. The proposed winery will be built on the abbey grounds.

For initial offerings, the grapes will be obtained from small growers in Fremont County and from other vineyards. Chardonnay and Riesling are expected to be among the initial offerings.

Let's Celebrate!

*E*ach year, on the third Saturday in September, the Colorado Mountain Winefest takes place in the Palisade town park. In 2001 more than 5,000 people showed up to sample wines, observe demonstrations, and enjoy music and dancing. This winefest is limited to Colorado wines, and many of the winemakers are present to greet the visitors. There are also banquets and winery tours during the weekend. The Colorado Mountain Winefest has been designated by the American Bus Association (which represents about 800 motorcoach operators in the United States and Canada) as one of the 100 top events in North America!

Another celebration of Colorado wines is held at Lafayette the third weekend in June. It includes a dinner, symphonic and other music, tastings, and seminars. Chefs from the Denver metropolitan area demonstrate their culinary preparations and suggest the wines that they feel will go best with their food.

The annual Telluride Wine festival is also held in June. It features international and domestic wines, including some Colorado labels. World-renowned chefs prepare five course lunches featuring ten different wines. There is also entertainment, tastings and seminars.

A third June festival is the famous *Food and Wine* magazine Classic which was formerly held in Snowmass, but is now held in Aspen. This affair has been going on for two decades and is very upscale featuring famous chefs and wines from around the world.

There is also talk of an upcoming wine festival at Thornton and perhaps some of the other Front Range cities will follow suit.

Grand Valley
Wine Tours

For those without transportation, or who want to sample many wines without risking a DUI citation, there are three operating tour services available in the Grand Junction area. They offer prestige stretch limousine service as well as less expensive and comfortable van tours. They will pick up passengers at several hotels.

For limousine service, call 970-858-8500. Luxury van service is available from Gisho Shuttle at 970-523-7662 or toll free at 1-888-226-5031. Jurassic Tours may be reached at 970-256-0884.

The participating wineries are Canyon Winds, Carlson Vineyards, Colorado Cellars, Grande River Vineyards, Plum Creek Cellars, Rocky Mountain Meadery, St. Kathyrn Cellars, and Two Rivers Winery.

Details are available on the internet at www.visitgrand-junction.com.

Appendix

Most Colorado wineries have a presence on the Internet. The official website of the Colorado Wine Industry Development Board includes a winery listing, regional maps, wine recipes, historical information, and upcoming events. This website can be found at www.coloradowine.com.

Additionally, some wineries maintain their own websites that may include the historical information, location, tasting room hours, a wine list, and on-line ordering capability. Those wineries, in alphabetical order, are as follows:

Aspen Valley Winery, www.aspenwine.com

Carlson Vineyards, www.carlsonvineyards.com

Corley Vineyards, www.corleyvineyards.com

Cottonwood Cellars, cottonwoodcellars.com

Garfield Estates Winery, www.garfieldestates.com

Grande River Vineyards, granderiverwines.com

Holy Cross Abbey, www.holycrossabbey.org

   (Abbey information only)

Mountain Spirit Winery, mountainspiritwinery.com

Old Town Winery, www.oldtownwinery.com

Rocky Mountain Meadery, www.wic.net/meadery

St. Kathryn Cellars, www.st-kathryn-cellars.com

Stoney Mesa Winery, www.stoneymesa.com

Surface Creek Winery, www.surfacecreek.com

Trail Ridge Winery, www.trailridgewinery.com

Two Rivers Winery, www.tworiverswinery.com

Acknowledgements

The author is indebted to the following people who gave invaluable assistance to the preparation of this work:

Dan and Eva Baharav, Baharav Vineyards, Carbondale.

Doug Caskey, Colorado Wine Industry Development Board, Boulder.

Horst Caspari, C.S.U. Orchard Mesa Research Station, Grand Junction.

Parker and Mary Carlson, Carlson Vineyards, Palisade.

Gene Corley, Corley Vineyards, Palisade.

Bill Donahue, Creekside Cellars, Evergreen.

Robert C. Dougherty, Editor, *Palisade Tribune*

Guy and Ruth Drew, Guy Drew Vineyards, Cortez.

Ted Dunn, Minturn Cellars, Minturn.

Jim Durr, Surface Creek Winery, Eckert.

David and Marschall Fansler, Rocky Hill Winery, Montrose.

Marisa Fay, Palisade.

Randy Fay, Denver.

Jane Foster, Palisade.

Alfred Goffredi, son of pioneer grower, Grand Junction.

Rick Gonzales, C.S.U. Orchard Mesa Station, Grand Junction.

Lindon Granat, early Vinelands orchardist, Palisade.

Mike and Barbara Heck, viticulturalists, Paonia.

Julia Herz, Redstone Meadery, Boulder.

Brian Hiebert, Mesa County Public Library, Palisade.

Gerald Ivancie, Littleton

Jill Judd, Lafayette.

Conrad Kindsfather, Old Town Winery, Aurora.

Doug Kinkle, Cobble Hill Vineyard, Palisade.

Patrick Leto, Aspen Valley Winery, Carbondale.

Cameron Lyeth, Canyon Winds Cellars and Garfield Estates, Palisade.

John and Joan Matthewson, Terror Creek Winery, Paonia.

Lydia and Bob Maurer, Gunnison

Tim Merrick, Trail Ridge Winery, Loveland.

Ulla Merz, Bookcliff Cellars, Boulder.

Jean Opsal, Palisade Chamber of Commerce

Judy Prosser-Armstrong, Museum of Western Colorado, Grand Junction.

Ron, Donna, and Brett Neal, Stoney Mesa Winery, Cedaredge.

Gaylene Ore, Ore Communications, Granby.

Eames and Pamela Petersen, Puesta Del Sol Winery, Paonia.

Sue Phillips, Plum Creek Cellars, Denver and Paonia.

Bennett and Davy Price, DeBeque Canyon Winery, Palisade.

Diana Read, Cottonwood Cellars, Olathe.

Steve Rhodes, S. Rhodes Vineyards, Hotchkiss.

Ann Seewald, who helped her late husband, Jim, in founding the Colorado wine industry, Grand Junction.

Joe Shield, Littleton.

Stephen Smith, Grand River Vineyards, Palisade.

June Spero, Spero Winery, Arvada.

Fred and Connie Strothman, Confre Cellars, Palisade.

John Sutcliffe, Sutcliffe Vineyards, Cortez.

Rick Turley, Colorado Cellars, Palisade.

Douglas Vogel, Reeder Mesa Vineyards, Whitewater.

Marianne "Gussie" Walters, Augustina's Winery, Boulder.

Sissi Savoya Williams, Museum of Western Colorado, Grand Junction.

Tom and Kate Williams, Steamboat Springs Cellars, Steamboat Springs.

Bob and Billie Witham, Two Rivers Winery, Grand Junction.

And a special thanks to my wife, Joan, for her help at every stage of the research and writing.

Bibliography

Adams, Leon D. *The Commonsense Book of Wines.* San Francisco, 1991.

Bender, Michael C. "Several New Wines from Two Rivers Winery are Award Winners." *Grand Junction Daily Sentinel,* May 18, 2001.

Briggs, Bill. "Less Mystery on the Vines." *Denver Post,* March 19, 2001.

Bunte, William Kirk. "A History of Rapid Creek." *Journal of the Western Slope,* Fall, 1994.

Castle, Phil. "Wine Country." *Business Times of Western Colorado,* May 2, 2001.

Colorado State University Cooperative Extension: *Fruit Growers Newsletter* (various issues related to wines)

Crawford, James. "Colorado's Only Winery Scores Silver Medal Cup." *Rocky Mountain News,* September 7, 1970.

Frank, Jerritt. "Women, Politics and Booze: Prohibition in Mesa County, 1908-1933." *Journal of the Western Slope,* Fall, 1999.

Friedrich, Jaqueline. "In France, A Vintners Revolt Born in a Garage." *Wall Street Journal,* May 8, 2001.

Gaitel, Dorothy J. and John Brecher. "Vintage Questions on Wine." *Wall Street Journal,* March 11, 2001.

Hamman, Richard, Jr. *Colorado Grape Growers Guide.* Fort Collins, 1996.

Lofholm, Nancy. "Bouquet of Vineyards Growing." *Denver Post,* Jan. 2, 2001.

Maracso, Sue Ann. "Transplanting the Body: Bringing Southern Italian Culture to Grand Junction, 1870-1933." *Journal of the Western Slope,* Spring, 1999.

Moloney, Michael. "A History of the Palisade Wine Industry." *A Journal of the Western Slope,* Spring, 1996.

Porter, Aaron. "Wineries in Delta County Get National Recognition." *Grand Junction Sentinel,* May 27, 2001.

Porter, Mary Jean. Series in *Pueblo Chieftain,* 2000-2001.

Rosen, Jennifer. "Trial by Terrior." *Palisade Tribune,* Sept. 13, 2001.

Smith, Alta and Brad. "Bottled in Colorado." *Denver's Mile High Magazine,* Oct.-Nov. 2000.

The Guide to Colorado Wines. Boulder, 1997.

Vader, Marija B. "Wine Industry Toasts Success." *Grand Junction Sentinel,* August 24, 2001.

Index